Please Note:-

Visits to the Doo Cave and Jonathan's Ca'

Entry to the Court, Sliding, Well and Gasworks Caves may not be advisable.

Those entering the Caves do so at their own risk

Index

Foreword

I would like to dedicate this book to the memory of Mr James Burt who took me on a guided tour of the Wemyss Caves over 30 years ago. I am sure he would have been very pleased to see the interest that has been shown in the Caves and would have been an active member of "Save Wemyss Ancient Caves Society".

Frank Rankin 1988

Introduction

There is an old legend that the caves were 'biggit by the Pechs, short wee men wi' red hair and lang airms and feet sae broad that when it rained they turned them up and they served as umbrellas. Oh aye they were graund builders the Pechs'.

Mr James Burt

But the geologists tell a different story. About 6000-7000 BC the sea formed a series of caves in the sandstone cliffs. Between this date and 3000-4000 BC, at the end of the last Ice Age, the land rose 8 metres and a series of caves were formed. The land then rose another 8 metres and another series of caves were formed, so that today there are two series of caves, one series 16 metres above sea level and the other 8 metres above sea level.

There are two or three caves at the 16 metres level under Wemyss Castle and the Red House and another was discovered under the boiler house at the Michael Colliery in 1929, in addition to the Glass Cave, once close to the Michael Colliery.

Location of the Caves

To reach the Caves, visit the village of East Wemyss, in Fife on the A955 road, 6 miles north of Kirkcaldy and 5 miles south of Leven.

Two roads lead to the Shore the first is between the cemetery and the Primary School at the north-end and the other is just past the 'Carshed', a newsagent on the east side of the road. Take the road downwards to the Shore and continue until reaching the Interpretation Boards just in front of Weavers Court.

Walk along the shore path in the direction of Buckhaven (north). Just past the car parking area is the large Court Cave; continue along the Shore passing the Doo Cave.

Due to recent coastal erosion one may either continue along the Shore via the sea wall or just past the Doo Cave take the path up the hill which to date (2001) is very wet, muddy, steep, and is in very poor condition. Continue around Macduff Castle and return to the Shore by Jonathan's "Road" a track that leads to the Shore from near the north gate of the Cemetery.

On the shore path one reaches Castle Green with Macduff Castle, once twin-towered now but a single tower rising high above the cliffs with the three Well Caves below.

Continue along the Shore until reaching Jonathan's Road which is part of the detour around by the Castle to Jonathan's Cave. If the tide is low continue along the Shore to the Sloping Cave, White Cove and Gasworks Cave, a total distance of about half a mile.

Professor Simpson's Visit 1865,1866

All over Scotland upright stone slabs have been discovered. These slabs were raised by the Picts and were decorated with symbols, pictures of animals and fish.

Up to the middle of the 19th Century the Pictish markings were thought to be funereal but in the summer of 1865 two Edinburgh gentlemen, Professor James Young Simpson (famous for the introduction of chloroform to relieve the pains of childbirth) and his friend Dr Dewar were on holiday in the Wemyss area. Professor Simpson, in addition to discovering chloroform was also a keen archaeologist.

In the 'Proceedings of the Antiquarian Society' of 1865. Professor Simpson described his hurried visit to the Caves and how he saw what he described as 'rude sculptures' in one of them.

He returned the next year for a further search with Drs Robertson, Dunn and Paterson and two or three new caves were visited.

The archaeological world sat up and took notice because here in the Wemyss Caves were markings similar to those on the Cross Slabs.

In fact there are more markings in the Wemyss Caves than in all the caves of Britain put together.

The only caves like them are the Covesea Caves on the Moray Firth and there are only two or three there and they are in a place very hard to reach.

16 Metre Level Caves

Glass Cave

Last century there was a large cave on the west side of the Michael Colliery named the Glass Cave.

In 1610, Sir George Hay, Lord Clerk to the Registrar and later Lord Kinnoul, established a glassworks in this cave. This was one of the earliest glassworks in Scotland. The work carried on at a considerable loss as the demand was not particularly heavy.

1619 Privy Council report to James VI: 'Income for glass for a year would not meet one month's bill at the works'.

1691 Works still active.

1698 David, Second Earl of Wemyss obtained an Act of Parliament to make certain kinds of glass.

1790 Mr Gibb, who was the Parish Minister, wrote, "This cave is 200 feet (60 metres) in length, 100 feet (30 metres) broad and about 30 feet (9 metres) in height. It was fitted up about 60 years ago by a tacksman for glassworks. Soon after work commenced, the man became bankrupt and the buildings were allowed to go into ruin.

In 1898 the Michael Colliery shafts were sunk a little to the east of the Cave. In the course of time the upper seams of coal were worked under the Cave and on an evening in 1901 the Cave collapsed and is now filled in with redd from the colliery.

This cave was often used by cattle as a shelter from the sun. It is also said to have had a chimney in the centre of the roof. The last hole of the Wemyss Golf Course lay at one of the entrances. A blocked up entrance can still be seen beside the Coastal Path which passes through the site of the old Michael Colliery.

Michael Cave

This Cave cannot be visited but was below the Colliery towards the west of East Wemyss village. It was discovered in 1929 when a new boiler was to be installed at the Michael Colliery. On investigation it was found that there was a big hole under where the new boiler was to be sited and that this led into a Cave.

The late Mr George Deas, (1875-1961) architect from Kirkcaldy, who was considered the Authority on the Wemyss Caves at that time was sent for and accompanied by another archaeologist, he inspected the Cave.

The entrance wall had been blocked up, but some markings were found on the walls. One of the markings was a 'Cup and Ring' which was believed to be a record of an astronomical event in the Bronze Age.

Another marking was pecked out on the wall and when the holes were joined with chalk, the drawing was revealed of a hunter sitting on his haunches. Over his head he wore a hood to deceive the Elk which stood or lay on his right. The hunter was aiming his bow and arrow over the heart of the beast, which was marked by a circle.

Mr Deas pleaded for a day or two's grace to examine this cave more fully as it had possibly never been opened since 1690, the latter being a date cut in the wall.

Unfortunately the boiler had to go into operation again as quickly as possible and all Mr Deas could do was to photograph the markings and leave the workmen to fill in the Cave with concrete.

Michael Cave Markings

Hunting scene

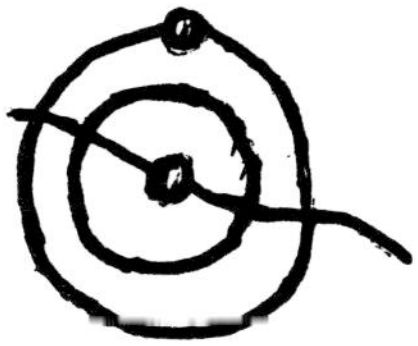

Concentric Cup and Ring

Self-guided Tour of the Caves - 8 metre Level

Interpretation Boards

On the shore by the Car Park area and the sea defence boulders are four interpretation boards telling the story of the Caves and their drawings. The posts are on a large area of rectangular setts in the shape of a double disc. There is also a board concerning the Coastal Path. Between the pairs of panels is a seat installed here in June 2000 by Save Wemyss Ancient Caves Society.

Court Cave

The first cave one comes to after leaving East Wemyss is the Court Cave. It is only a few metres past the Car Park and boulders.

In the middle ages the land owner was responsible for the upkeep of law and order and he presided over the 'Baron's Courts' which were normally held in the open air.

The owners of the Wemyss Estates were fortunate in having the magnificent cave in which to hold their courts. The court was summoned by ringing a bell which hung from the mouth of the Cave. Before the front of the Cave collapsed in 1970 the marks made by the bell-rope could be seen.

Others have traced the Cave's name from the days when James V, disguised as the 'Guidman of Ballangiech', had an incident with the gypsies who were staying in the Cave at this time.

This Cave has two large entrances and two passageways, one a short one through the end of which was an opening so that the ladies from Wemyss who gutted the herring in Buckhaven could walk home safely when the tide was high. This passageway was later used to carry the gas pipe from the Macduff Gasworks along the shore to the village. The other was at the back of the Cave and was said to lead to

Kennoway, three miles away. However there has been a fall here and the floor rises to the roof, about 20 metres in.

Five brick pillars were built into the Cave by the Wemyss Coal Company in 1934, to prevent the collapse of this famous cave due to mining works from the Michael Colliery below the ground. When the front of the Cave collapsed in 1970, one of the pillars was demolished, almost blocking the main entrance. There was a further small fall in 1990 when a tree fell from the cliff above the entrance.

The Cave has also been called the Piper's Cave because of the legend that a piper was said to have marched into the Cave playing his pipes and was never seen again ! Another name given was 'Barque Cove' because the fisherman used to barque their nets in this Cave.

Ghost of the Court Cave - the White Lady

Mary Sibbald the daughter of the Laird of Balgonie Castle died in the Well Cave under tragic circumstances.

Mary fell in love with one of the gypsies and eloped with him. The gypsy's previous girl friend was jealous and set Mary up, planting a piece of her jewellery below Mary's sleeping mat and declared that someone had stolen her brooch. A hunt was made and the brooch was found beneath Mary's mat. She was sentenced by the Baron Baillie of Wester Wemyss to be whipped twelve times. Mary was a lady with refined and gentle manners and she felt the indignity keenly. She died of a broken heart in the Well Cave when the Prior of St Mary's Chapel by-the-sea was applying healing waters to her wounds from the well which at that time bubbled up in the Well Cave.

On two occasions of the visit of the Guidman, a quarrel arose among the gypsies, by one accused of bearing false witness against the young girl. "You were the thief" were the words which rang through the Cave above the Royal and other tongues and as the culprit sat with the lie on her lips, a female clad in white suddenly appeared. The unearthly visitor disappeared as quickly as she had come, but her visit was long enough to strike terror in the hearts of the gypsies and before many minutes had elapsed they quitted the Cave, while the King made for the Castle. "A lady with large soft blue eyes" was the King's description of the unearthly visitor. The Baron Baillie started at the description, for the same eyes had haunted him since the eventful morning of the trial in the Court Cave. The King and the Baron Baillie were agreed that the apparition must have been that of Mary Sibbald. The ghost haunted the gypsies until the real thief confessed her guilt.

Even after Jean Lindsey had been brought to boot, the White Lady makes occasional appearances around the Castle and the Court Cave, today.

Entrance to the Court Cave 1996

On the west wall is a long undulating line which begins near the entrance and finishes in a fancy tail. The late George Deas, the authority on the Caves in his time believed it may have represented a 12 metre serpent of unknown date.

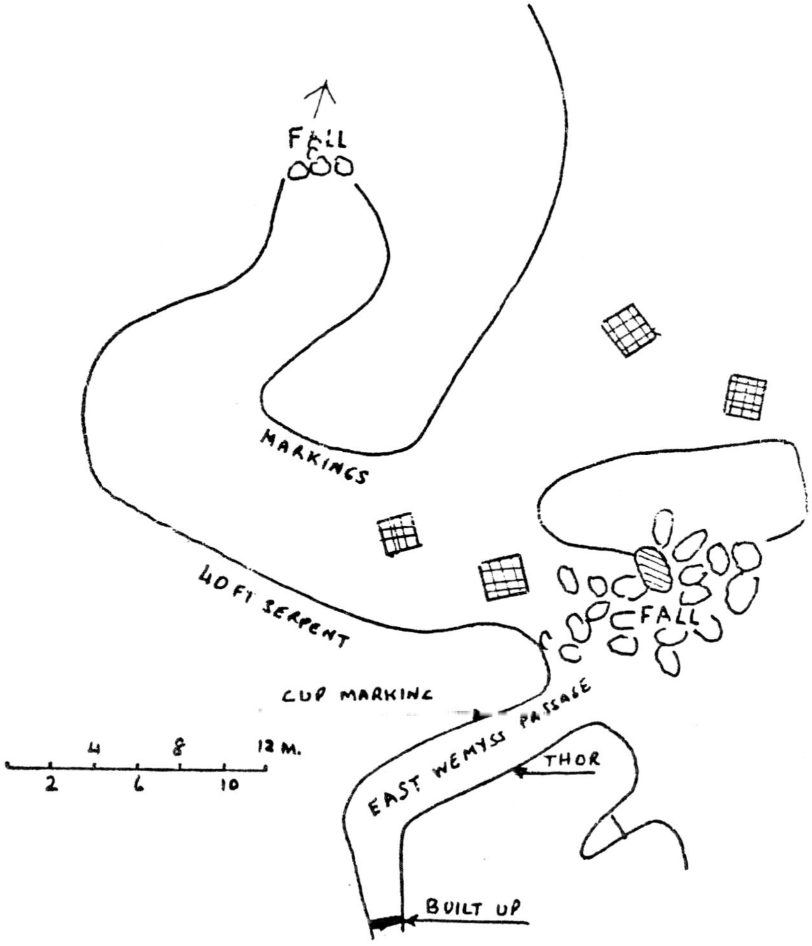

Plan of the Court Cave

Court Cave Markings

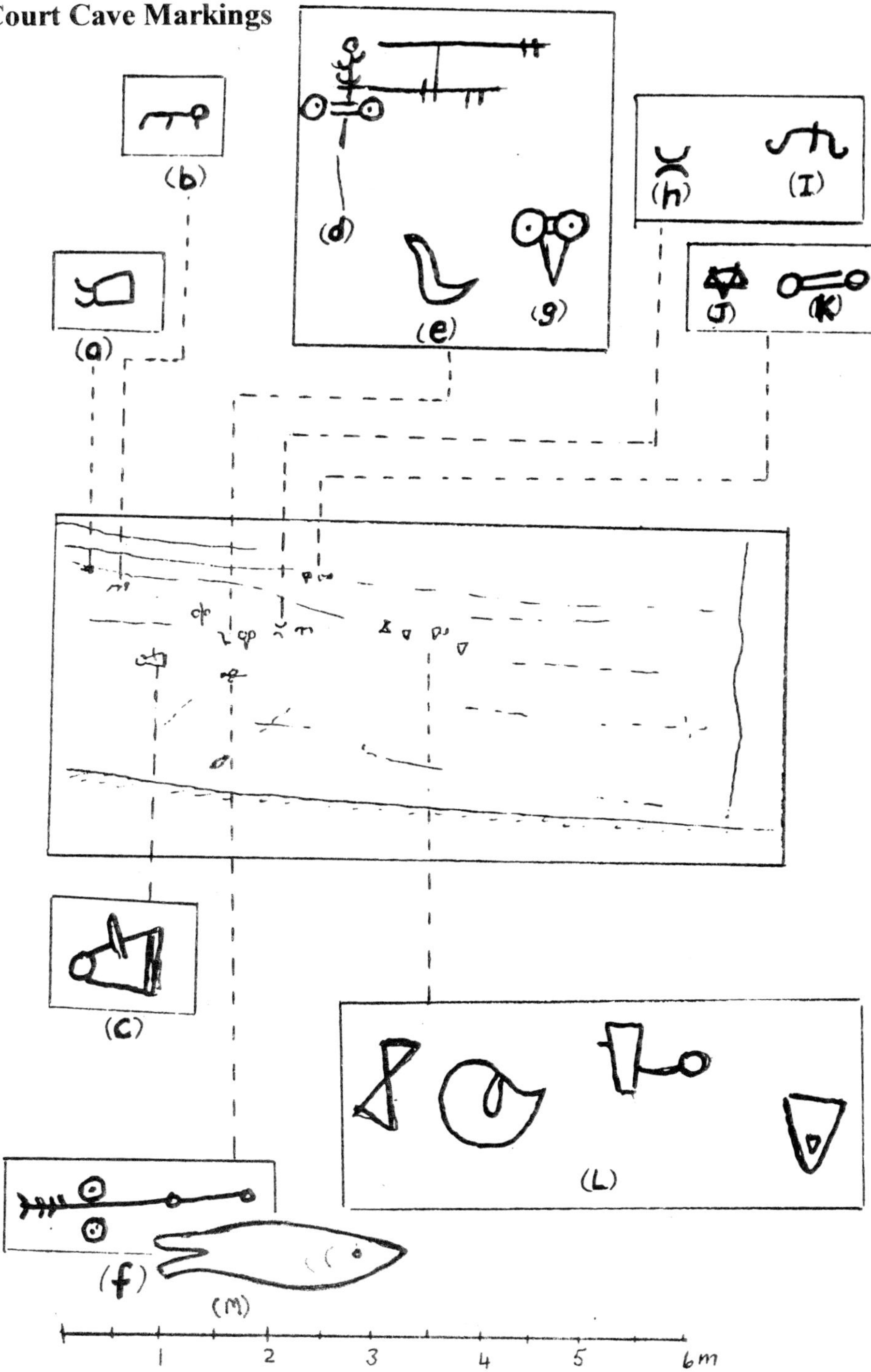

Court Cave Markings

In the East Wemyss passage are two markings:-

This marking on the south wall is possibly of the Viking god Thor with his hammer and sacred goat. Dates 800-900 AD

Directly across the passage are these cup marks. There are various theories as to their meaning It has been suggested that they are calendars, fertility symbols, charms for extracting metal ore from the ground or rock maps. Date 1000-3000BC

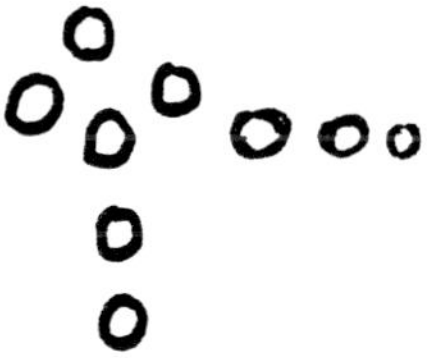

On the east wall of the main cave are the following:-

This marking is very feint. Meaning unknown.

This marking is also very feint. It is known as an 'elephant figure' because of its similarity to the 'elephant figures' on the Pictish sculptured stones.

(a)

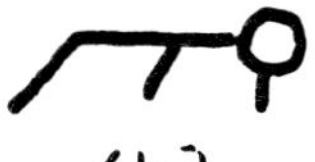

(b)

This marking is said to represent a Pictish brooch with the latch on the right side. This too is becoming feint.

(c)

This marking depicts a double disc or florinated rod or sceptre. Because the shaft of the sceptre is broken it is believed that it probably denotes the death of a person in authority. The vertical marks on the horizontal lines may be related to Ogham script found on many northern Pictish stones and in Jonathan's Cave.

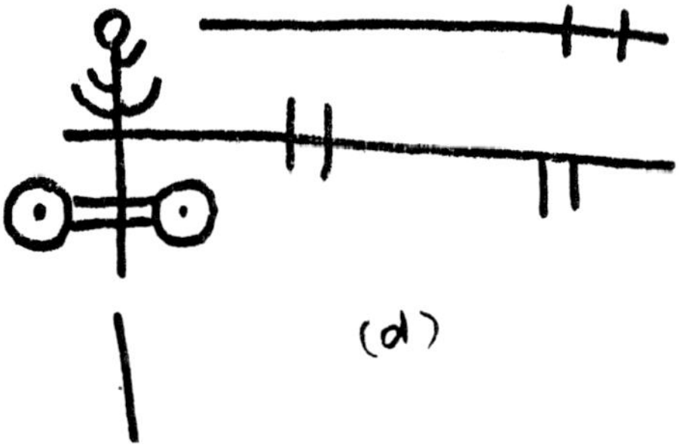

(d)

A long-necked bird, possibly a goose.

(e)

(f)

Another double disc and florinated rod, probably denoting a person in authority.

A double disc and V-rod.

(g)

A double crescent.

(H)

Another 'elephant figure' which some experts believe represents Viking scales. Most Viking symbols are of gods or justice. Date if Viking : 800-900 AD

(I)

This marking is very feint and depicts a crescent and V-rod

(J)

This marking is also very feint and depicts a double disc, the right hand one being double.

(K)

A group of unidentified makings.

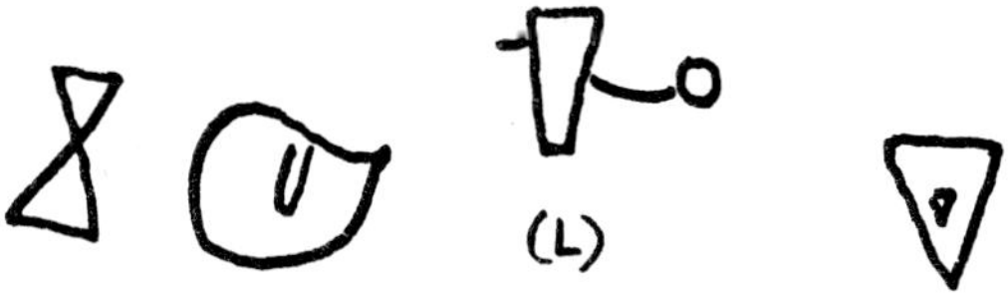

(L)

A leaping salmon.

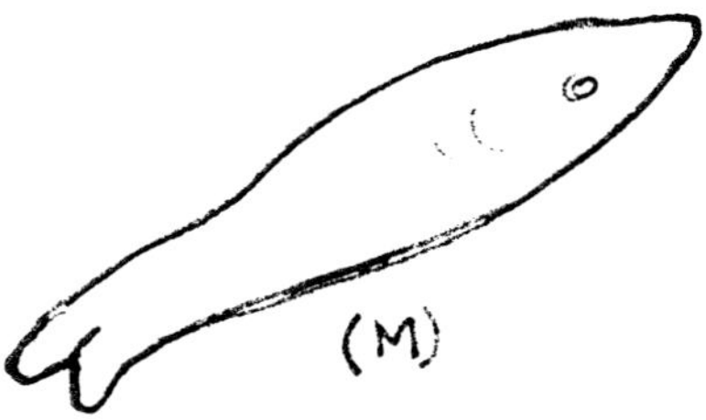

(M)

Doo Caves

In the Middle Ages only lairds and burghs were allowed to keep pigeons to provide fresh meat during the winter months when many of the cows had to be slaughtered and the meat salted as there was not enough hay for all the cattle to survive the winter. It was only when Charles Townshend discovered (c1735) that the turnip was a suitable winter feed that doocots gradually died out.

Pigeons and pigeon lofts were often included in the dowry for the laird's daughters. It is said that at one time four of the caves had been set up as pigeon houses as well as the Doocot which once stood near the Shore but has since been washed away. Before the First World War there were two Doo Caves, the East and the West. Holes for the pigeon to fly in and out were built high above the bricked-up entrances. Entry to the East Doo Cave was from a passageway at the side and similarly on the west side of the West Doo Cave. These two caves were interconnected by a passageway.

The **West Doo Cave** contained a number of markings which have thankfully been recorded in the 'Proceedings of the Antiquarian Society'. Sadly the West Doo Cave collapsed during the First World War when there was a battery above these caves and guns were frequently fired. All that is left now is a big hollow above and to the side of the East Doo Cave.

On counting the pigeon boxes in the **East Doo Cave** there were found to be 92, however with silting up of the floor now only about 70 can be counted, some doubles. Pigeons still nest in the Cave but only on the high ledges. Mud from the collapsed West Doo Cave ran down the connecting passage into the East Doo Cave so that the floor of the Cave now rises at the back. There is also a small seepage of water down the west side making a deep gulley. In 1945 a fierce storm washed away the sea wall and the grassy bank in front of the Cave broke down the wall which sealed off the entrance to the East Doo Cave so that the Cave is now open to the shore. There are no markings in this Cave.

Doo Cave

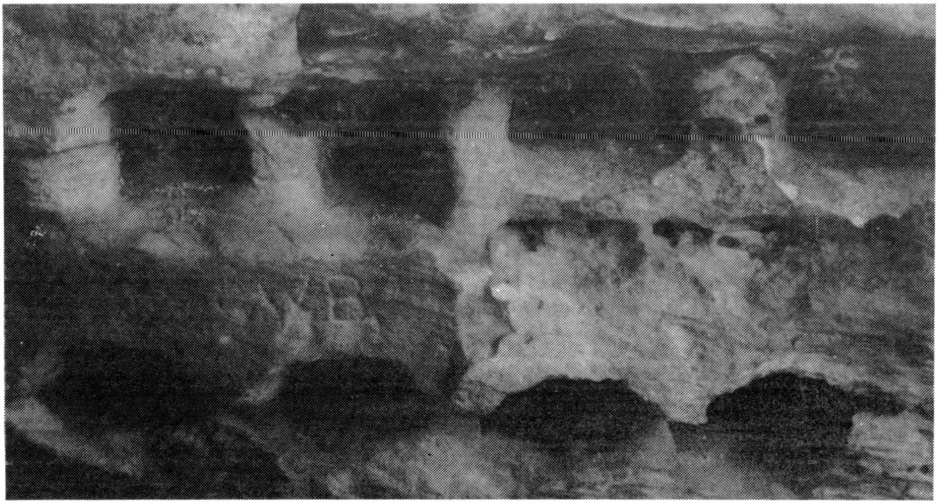

Pigeon "boxes' in the Doo Cave

West Doo Cave markings

a. Drawing of a dog.

b. This group depicts the Norse gods Thor (the trumpet form), Freya (the geese) and Odin (the F-figure).
The crosses are Christian symbols Date 800-900AD

c. Sun arches with single and double discs and other unidentified markings.

d. Two double discs and other unidentified markings.

e. and f. A double disc and other unidentified markings.

g. A double disc and z-rod with a horse's head beneath. A similar drawing on a silver link was found in a cairn at Norrie's Law in 1819 and is now in the Museum of Antiquities, Edinburgh.

h. A flower-like object.

i. A mirror.

j. A serpent.

k. A jug.

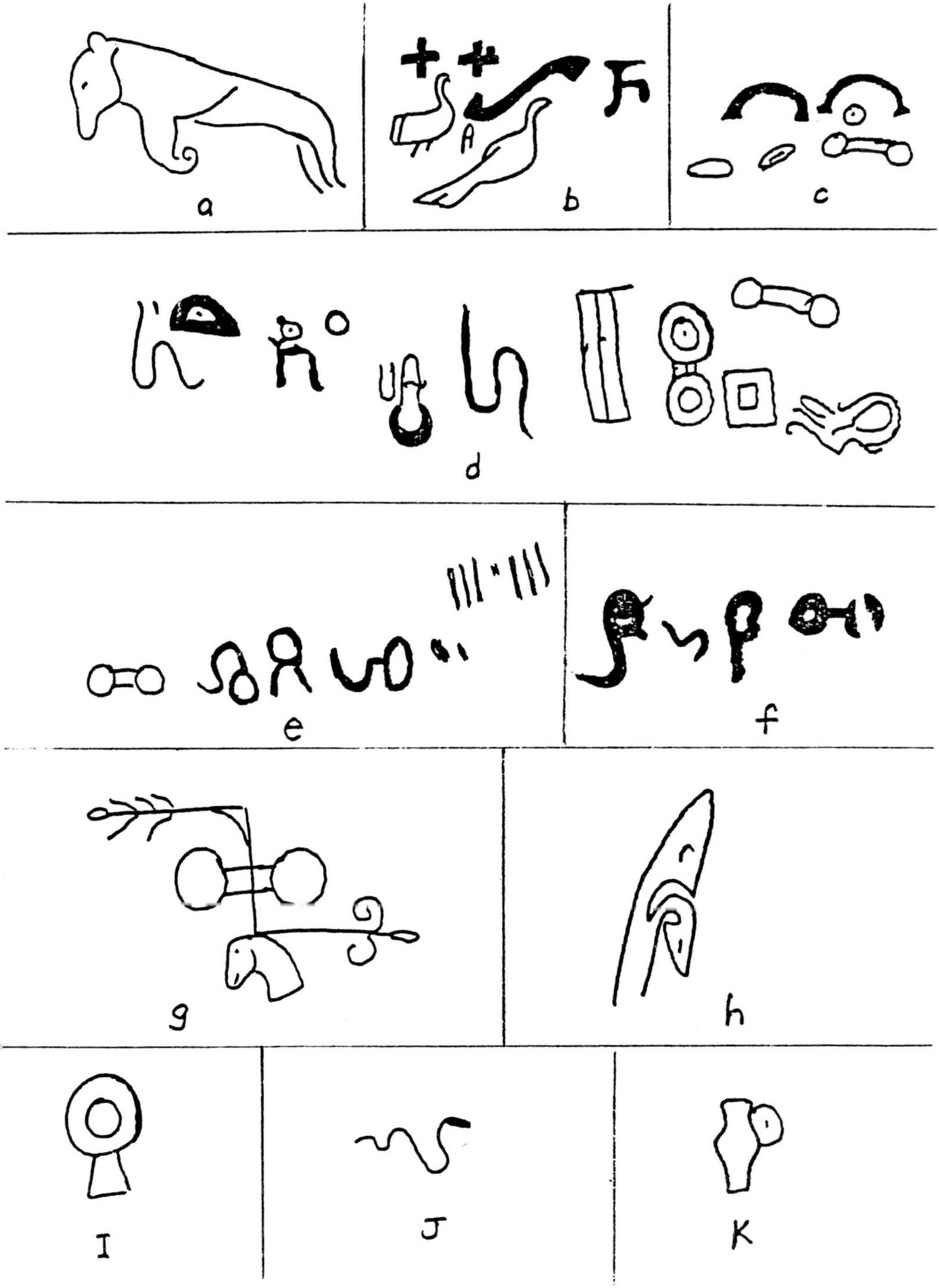
a
b
c
d
e
f
g
h
I
J
K

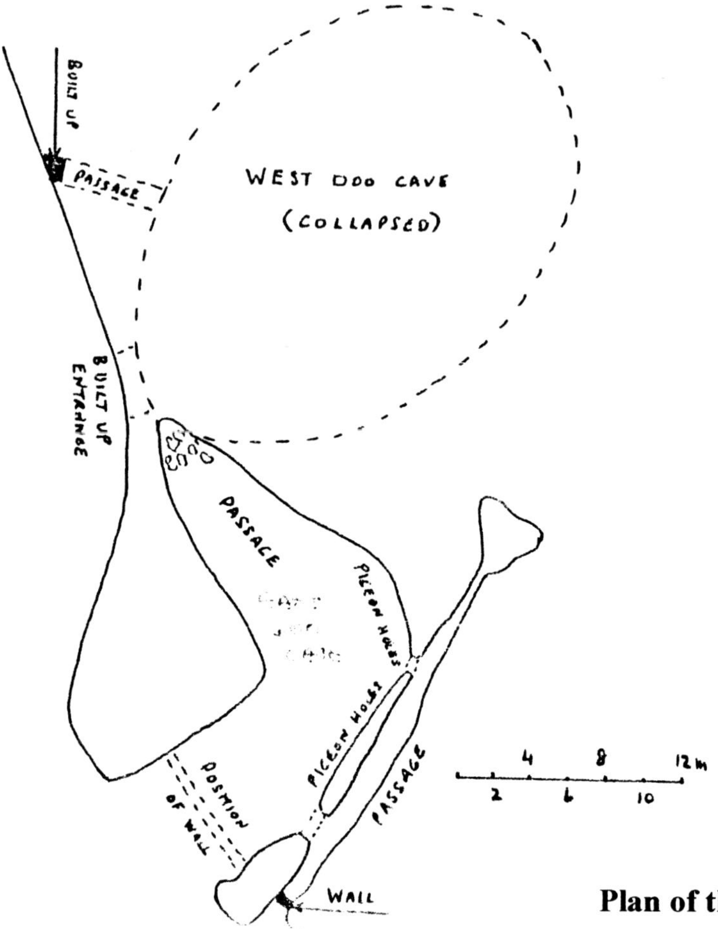

Plan of the Doo Caves

On leaving the Doo Cave one can follow the Shore around to 'Castle Green' walking a short distance along the old sewer wall or alternatively one can take the slippery path up the hill, around the back of Macduff Castle and return to the Shore via Jonathan's 'Road', a track which leads down to Jonathan's Cave. This was once the road used for supplies to the Gasworks.

Before taking either path one may see on the right on the path leading up the hill, an entrance to what might appear to be another cave. This however has not yet opened up.

The Doocot

Further east at the foot of the "Aberhill" was once a cylindrical 16th Century Doocot.

It was about 8 metres high, with an internal diameter of 4 metres, with the walls being 0.66 of a metre thick. It had a conical stone roof with a central opening for the birds and was lit by a window in the south. It stood high and dry on a grassy bank behind the sea wall.

Unfortunately after the sea wall was destroyed by the 1945 storm, the Doocot was exposed to the waves and over the years suffered damage which caused its final collapse in July 1986. Even the stones have now all been removed.

Doocot c. 1970

Map of the Wemyss

Scale Approx.

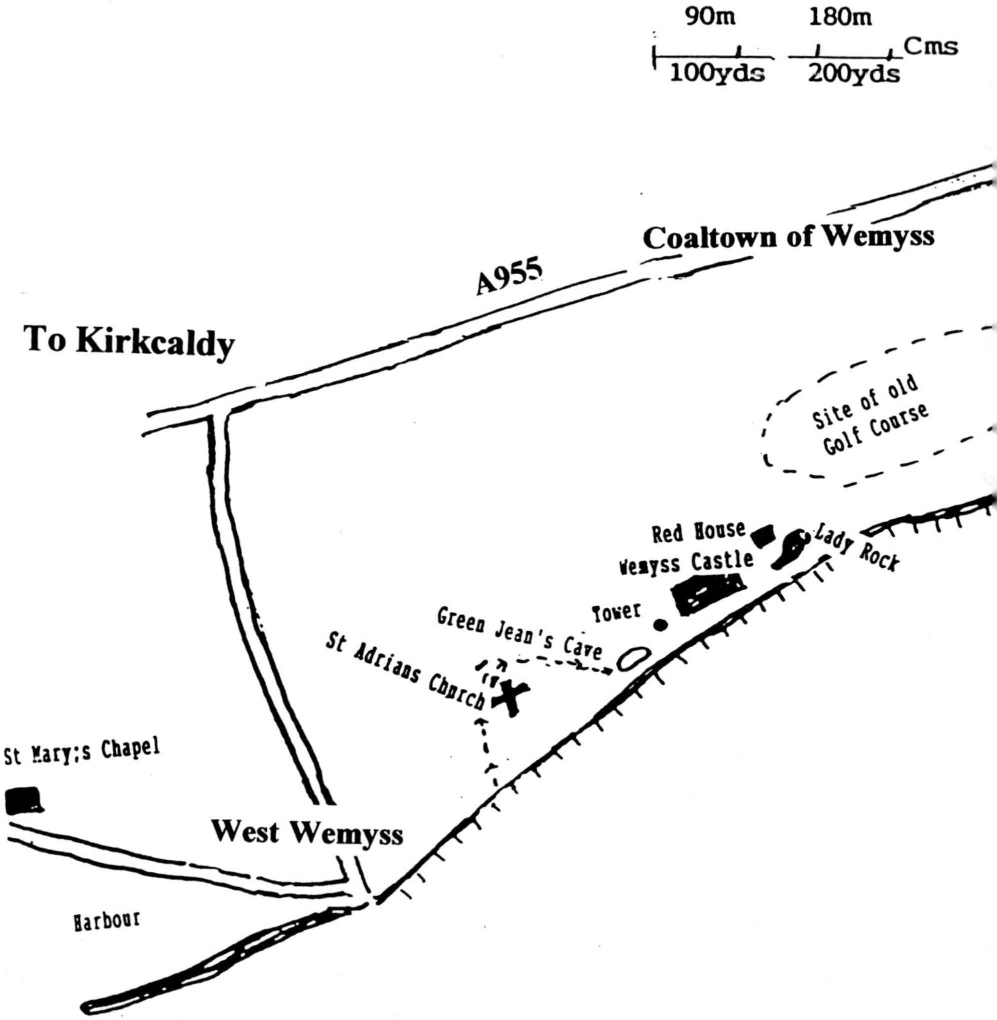

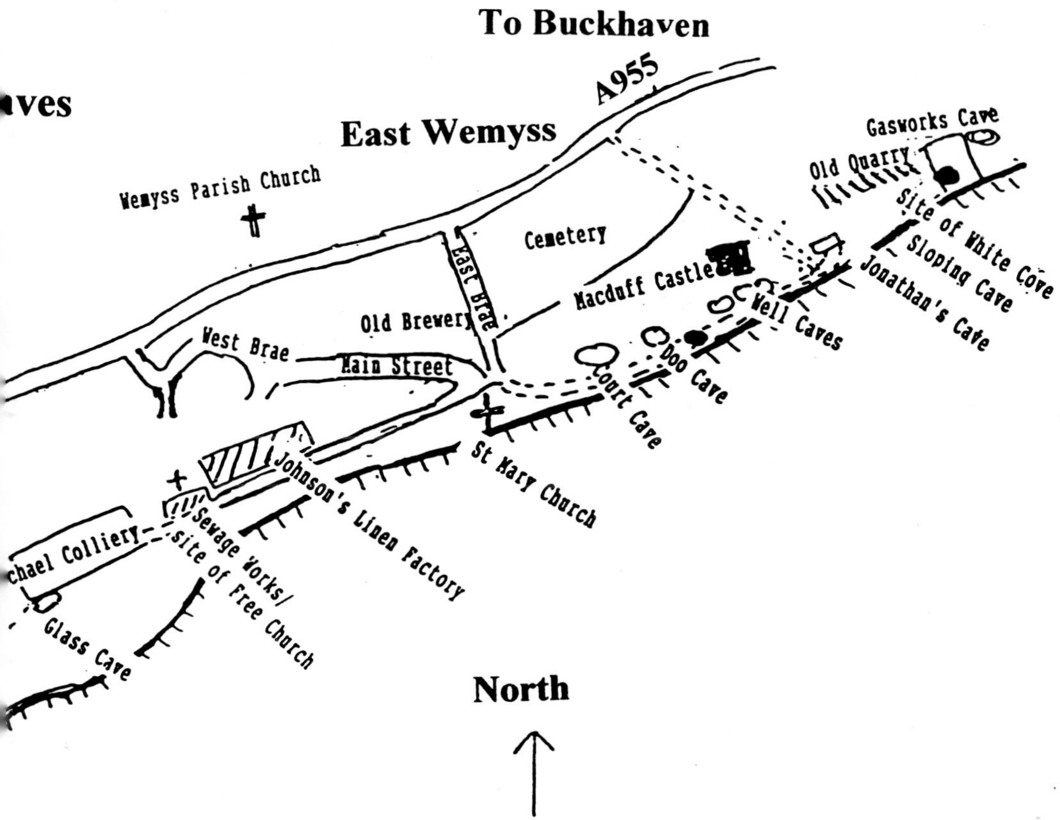
To Buckhaven
A955
East Wemyss
aves
Wemyss Parish Church
Cemetery
Gasworks Cave
Old Quarry
Site of White Cove
Sloping Cave
Jonathan's Cave
Macduff Castle
Well Caves
Doo Cave
Court Cave
East Brae
Old Brewery
West Brae
Main Street
St Mary Church
Johnson's Linen Factory
chael Colliery
Sewage Works/
site of Free Church
Glass Cave
North

Macduff Castle 1930

Macduff Castle from the air 1930

Macduff Castle

Macduff Castle can be reached by carefully going up the steep wet path from the Doo Cave or more easily by taking Jonathan's Road just before Jonathan's Cave, walking up and following the path round the side of the Cemetery.

Originally Macduff Castle must have been a wooden structure as stone castles were not built in Scotland until around the 13th Century. Macduff, Thane of Fife, who died around 1090, probably had several castles in order to visit all the parts of his 'kingdom'. Also it was customary to leave one castle and move to another so that it could be properly cleaned out. The first stone Macduff Castle may have been built by Ian Mor Nan Uamh, who died in 1265, commonly known as "Muckle John of the Caves". The remains of the stone walls can be seen by looking upwards above the Well Cave.

In 1304 Edward I, the Hammer of the Scots visited the Castle but it was not grand enough for him and when he found that Sir Michael was supporting Robert the Bruce he ordered the Castle to be burned. However all was not lost for in 1330 the Laird of Wemyss was entertaining Randolph, Earl of Moray in his Castle.

The Castle originally had twin towers and was surrounded by a wall. It was impossible to approach from the shore and so was defended from the landward side. Sadly in 1967 Fife County Council decided that the western tower was unsafe and ordered it to be demolished. It lies there under the grass.

The Castle was last said to be inhabited by the Duchess of Sutherland in 1666 when she came to Wemyss with her children to escape the plague. The Castle was repaired in 1926 and used as a store by the owners, the Wemyss family.

It is thought that Macduff's wife and family were killed by Macbeth, when Macduff was away. When he returned he was locked in his own dungeon. He knew his Castle and escaped down a flight of stairs which led down the passage into the Well Cave from where he moved along the coast to the "Earlsferry", so named as after he stayed in another cave there, known as Macduff's Cave, he (the Earl) was ferried across the water to obtain help.

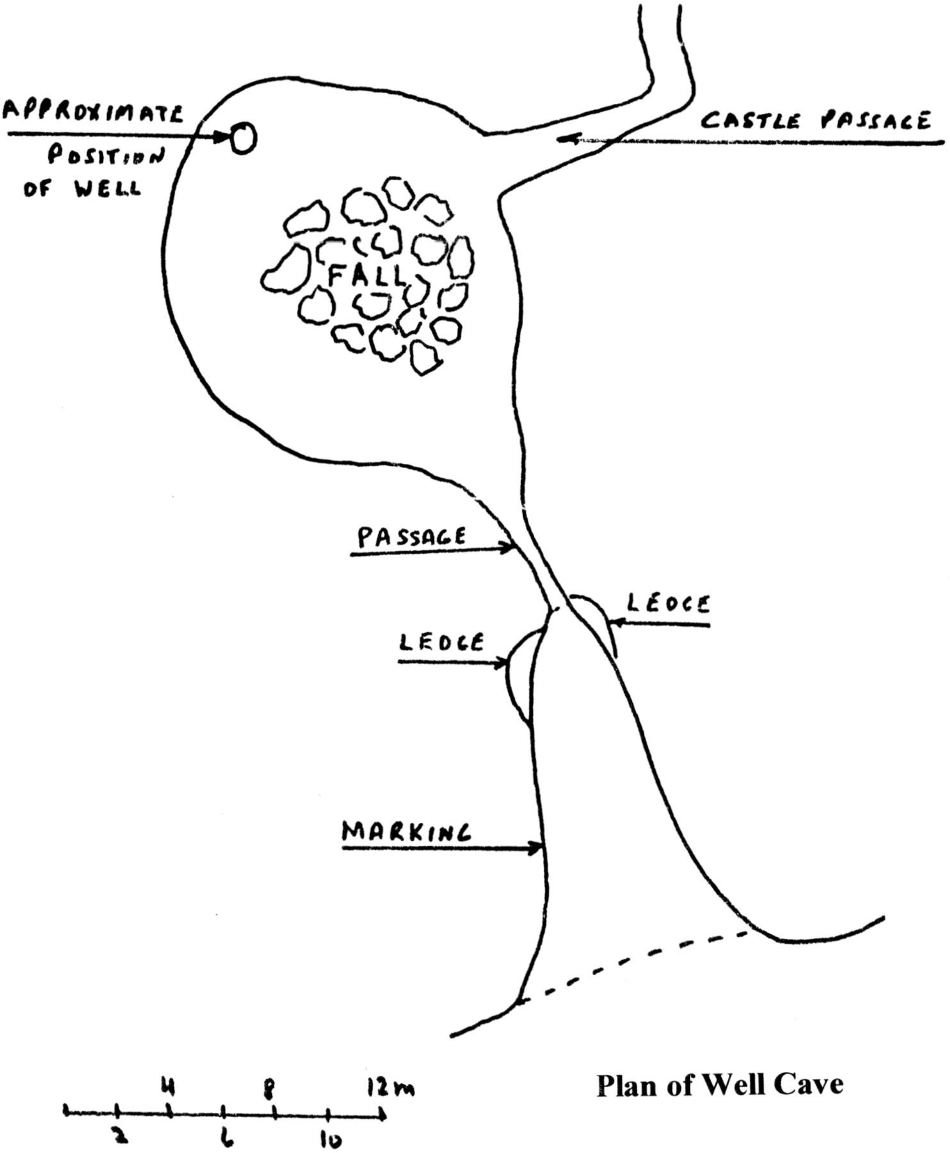

Plan of Well Cave

The Well Caves

On the broad semi-circle of grass below Macduff's Castle, "Castle Green" are the three Well Caves.

First is the **Fern Cave** - merely an entrance hollow, which has been filled in by soil and sand over the years and has not been opened up. Maybe there are more drawings inside.

Then there is a double cave the **Well Cave**. A 13 metre entrance cave connected by a very low 5 metre under-passage to the main Well Cave which is a large high cave, 20 metres long, 17 metres broad and with a high domed roof 8-10 metres above the floor. Iron bars have been placed between the floor and the roof to support the roof and a cloth laid on the floor to ascertain how much is falling from the roof. It is mainly a fine sand. This cave received its name because it contained a well of clear water which was said to have great curative powers. It is possible that the Well was there in the days of the Picts and would have been their local water supply. It was the reason for the Hansel Monday celebrations, a custom of the young people from the village of East Wemyss on what was then the first Monday after the New Year. There was a torchlight parade of young people to the Cave, when everyone sang hymns and songs around the Well. Cake and wine was then enjoyed by all and finally everyone had a drink of the water from the Well which it was hoped would protect them from any ill health during the coming year.

When Christianity came to Scotland the custom was 'Christianised' and the Well was named St Margaret's Well.

Before 1756 Hansel Monday was the first Monday after New Year but when the Gregorian Calendar was adopted this removed 11 days from the year in September and so Hansel Monday was the first Monday after January 11. The Scots were very angry about this and shouted loudly to no avail "Give us back our 11 days"!!

Entrance to the Well Cave with the grille

This Hansel Monday could have been the continuation of the old Celtic Halloween or 'Samhain' when the fairy piper was said to come to the caves to summon the wicked and when 'Tir Nan Og' wiled away the mortals to the land of eternal youth.

In the days of the Picts, the well was the mother of the spring, the spring was the mother of the river and the river flowed down to the sea and so the well was worshipped.

There are three very old framed pieces of graffiti on the east wall of the inner chamber dated 1866. However when examined with a video light the entire wall is covered with initials, one would presume these were done by members of the torchlight procession. There are no Pictish markings in the inner Well Cave and the only marking is on the west wall of the entrance cave but it is very hard to discern this bone-like marking. The Well Cave was connected to the East Tower of Macduff Castle, which was demolished in 1967, by a passageway leading from the back of the inner cave to a flight of steps up and into the Castle. The passageway is silted up and cannot be penetrated. However many older people in the village have recalled when these steps were visible, from the lower part of the now demolished tower.

The Well itself consists of some stones that glisten and are wet. Any deposit is salty. However the water course outside the Cave has changed. Recently the Well has suffered from a small roof-fall.

In 1992 a locked grille was placed over the mouth of the Cave. However vandals broke the lock and it now remains unlocked. SWACS had the grille painted in 1999.

Bone-like Marking

Unnamed Cave

To the right (north) of the Well Cave and a few metres from its opening, is the entrance is the third well cave, known as the **Unnamed Cave**. It has a low entrance, which leads downwards into a passageway about 18 metres long and is dry. There are no markings in this Cave. The west wall will not be far from the east wall of the Well Cave.

Unnamed Cave Plan **Scale 0.5 cms = 1 metre**

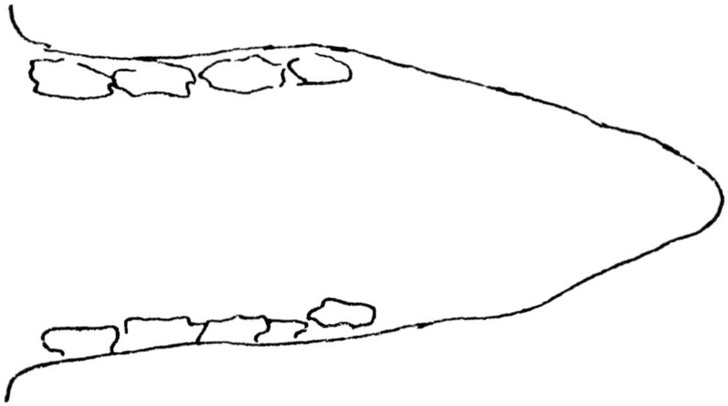

Elevation

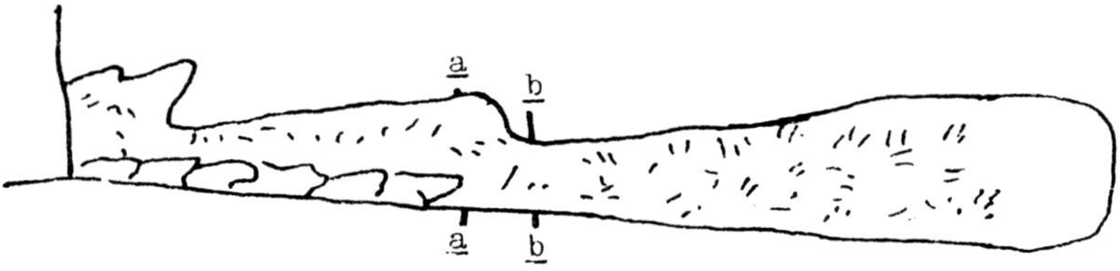

Section a-a **Section b-b**

Jonathan's Cave.

The next cave one reaches is Jonathan's Cave which is over 20 metres in length and has two large entrances. This cave has many interesting drawings.

At the rear of the Cave is a bench-like seam of rock which was said to be Jonathan's bed. Indeed the Picts would spread dry heather here and yarn away during the long winter nights.

Jonathan was a nail-maker who lived in this cave with his wife and children in the 18th Century. This form of hand-making of iron nails died out towards the end of the 18th Century due to more modern methods of nail-making introduced by the Carron Iron Company which set up near Falkirk in 1759 and closed around 1984. At one time old nails could be found on the floor of the Cave.

Another name for this cave has been the Factor's Cave and the Factor of Wemyss Castle Estate would use this cave to collect rents. It has also been seen on old maps as the Cat Cave.

This cave contains more markings than all the other caves here. All the markings are on the west wall with the exception of the ship which is on a bulge at eye level on the east wall, at the back of the Cave, but it is a little hard to discern now.

Sadly the drawing of a swan was destroyed in 1985 when a car was driven down Jonathan's Road and set on fire in the Cave. The Swan was a symbol of the Wemyss Family. This incident resulted in a grille being erected over the two entrances to Jonathan's Cave in 1988.

The Coastal Path from East Wemyss was washed away in 1993/94 and the vandals finally broke the lock and stole the padlock many times. The gate remains open, but sadly it has now rusted and dropped into the Cave. In 1999 SWACS had the grille painted as it was badly eroded. Sadly although supervised by Fife Council, a very poor job was done and the rust is again coming through.

Jonathan's Cave 1996

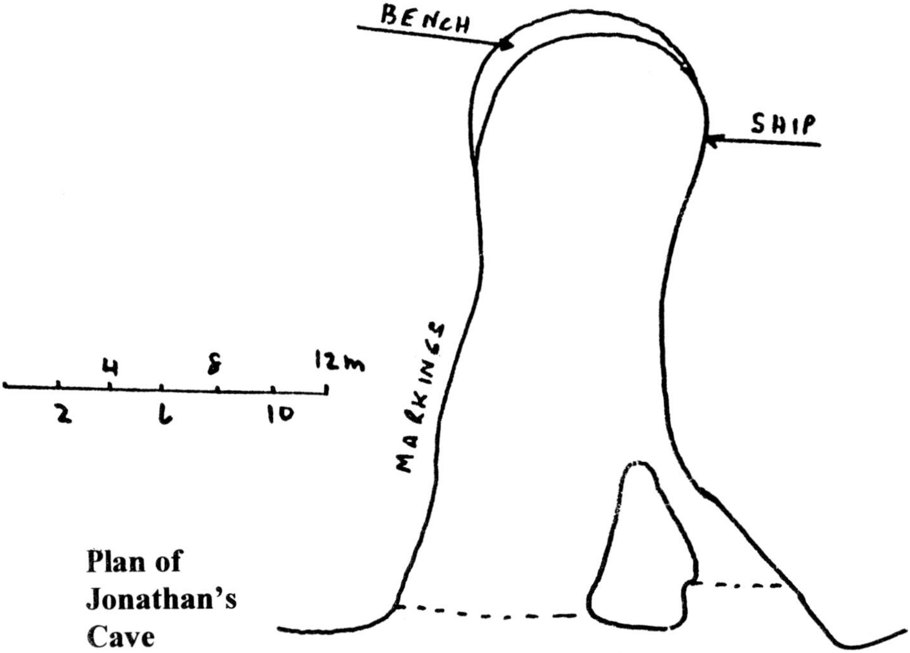

Plan of Jonathan's Cave

Markings in Jonathan's Cave

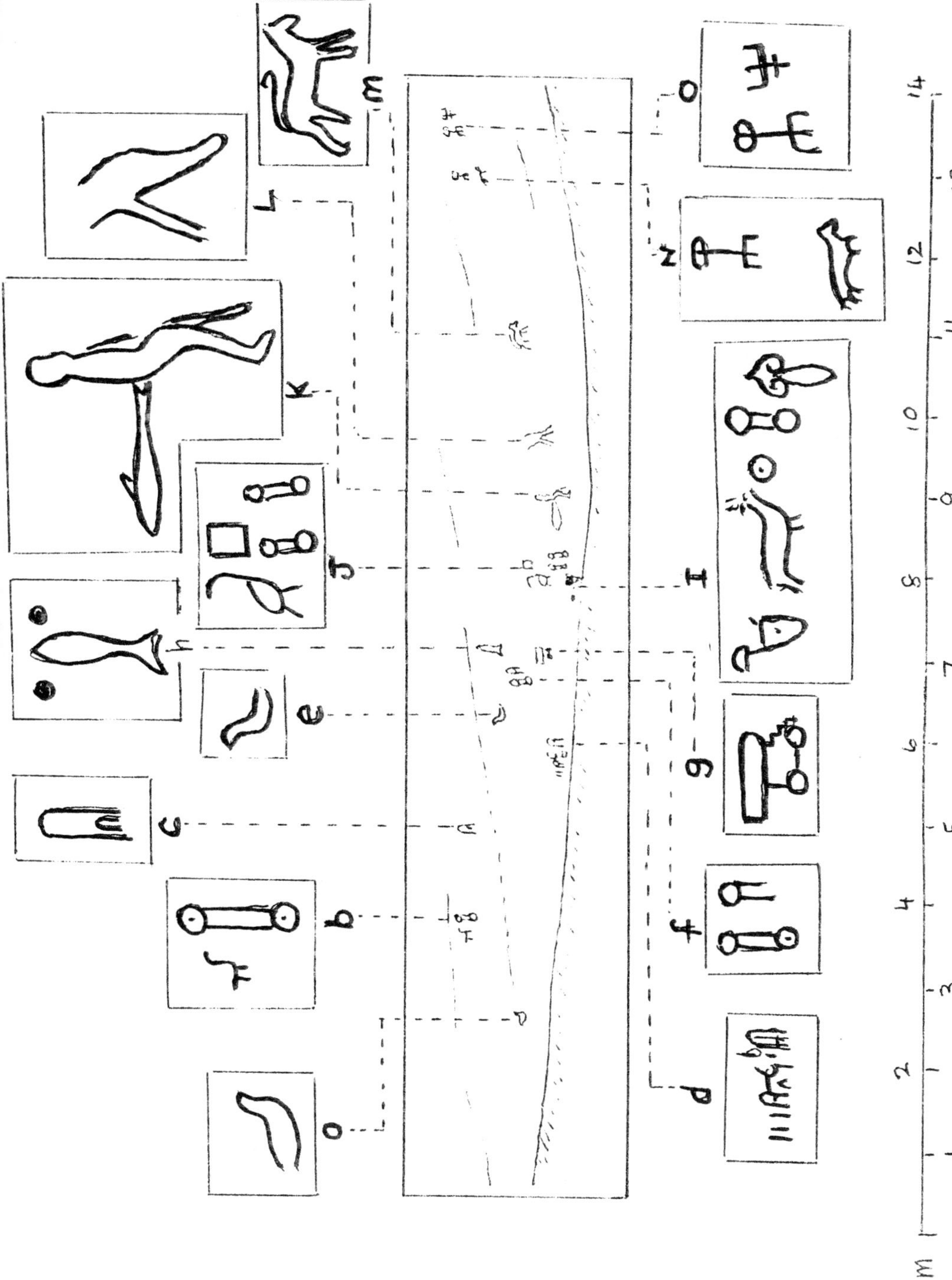

This marking is very feint. It may be a representation of a duck or goose.

(a)

This group depicts a double disc with a bird pointing to the top of the disc.

(b)

This 'elephant figure' may be a representation of a primitive hut. It is said that our ancestors only stayed in the caves during the winter and made huts for themselves in the summer.

(c)

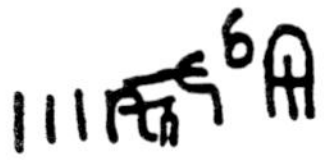

(d)

This is a group unidentified markings.

(e)

This a marking similar to (a) a bird or goose.

(f)

This is a pair of double discs.

This marking is not a 'Medieval Cannon'. According to Mr George Deas the original double disc marking (the wheels) has been added to during modern times. On close inspection it is obvious that the rest of the 'cannon' has been made with a penknife.

(g)

The drawing of a fish is quite common on Sculptured Stones It is an early Christian symbol. from the Greek work icthus, the letters meaning 'Jesus Christ Our Saviour'. At the head of the fish are two cup marks.

(h)

This group includes a dagger, a double disc and a single disc. The deer is now unrecognisable and the meaning of the other markings are unknown.

(I)

Two double discs below a square with a long-necked bird, possibly a swan on the left.

(J)

This is the drawing of a human figure, alongside a fish. Mr James Burt, who showed me round the caves many years ago said that the fish had been marked in modern times probably with a penknife.

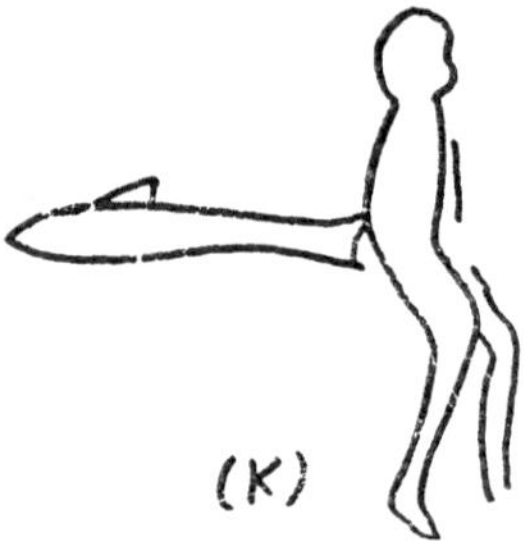

(K)

Opposite is the drawing of what might look like a bird. However the head may have worn away and someone has put an eye in the leg. In between the two drawings, best in certain lights, is seen a Pictish beastie.

(L)

This is a drawing of a horse with its tail flicked over its back.

(M)

This is a drawing of a dog or wolf. Above it is a 'trident' This was used for catching fish from the shallow waters.

(N)

Two more tridents, one upside down and the other without a handle.

(O)

Early Christian crosses of which there are several, some with blobs on the ends of the crosses. Date 800 AD.

This is the oldest drawing of a ship in Scotland. It was described and recorded by Mr George Deas, Architect in Kirkcaldy who was regarded as an expert on the Wemyss Caves in his time. Mr Deas made some castings of this marking and presented these to Kirkcaldy Museum, the Museum of Antiquities in Edinburgh and the Maritime Museum in Greenwich.

This marking at the back of the Cave on a bulge in the east wall probably depicts a Viking Trader or a Pictish ship, which if Viking would be dated between 800-900 AD.

On the roof at the back of the Cave on an overhanging ledge are some perpendicular lines said to be Pictish writing, Ogham's script. It has not been interpretative.

Unfortunately the swan and elephant figures were destroyed in 1986 when vandals pushed a car into Jonathan's Cave and set it on fire, causing the rock surface to flake off. This act of vandalism highlighted the need to preserve this historic site and resulted in the formation of the Save the Wemyss Ancient Caves Society, SWACS, which is working for the preservation of the Caves and their unique markings

Sloping Cave

Since the high seas of 1995/96 the Sloping Cave has opened up to the Shore and is no longer sloping.

Beyond Jonathan's Cave, approached via the Shore at low tide or the high rock path if not, this cave is found near the start of the old quarry. The Cave is about 6 metres in length, about one and a half metres in width and about 2 metres in height. On the east wall are two drawings boxed in. One is described as a mirror and the other as a comb-case. These were said to denote the death of a woman of authority. There are one or two hold fasts in this cave.

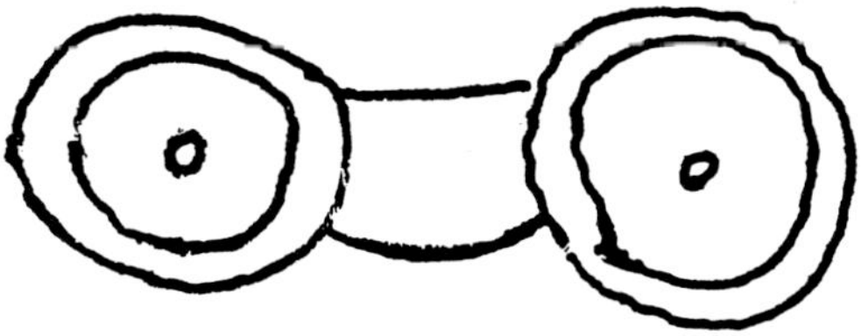

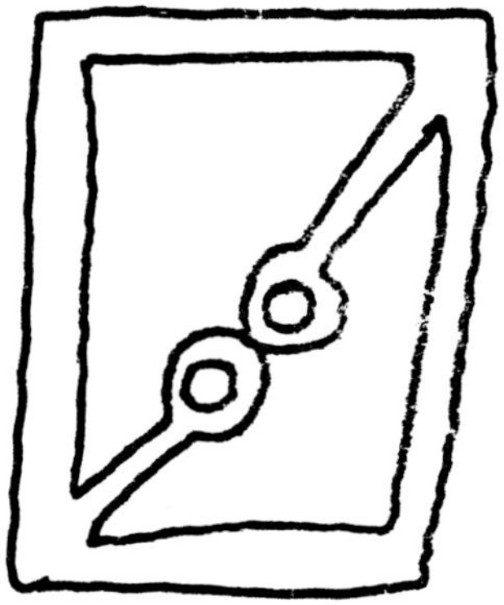

Comb-case

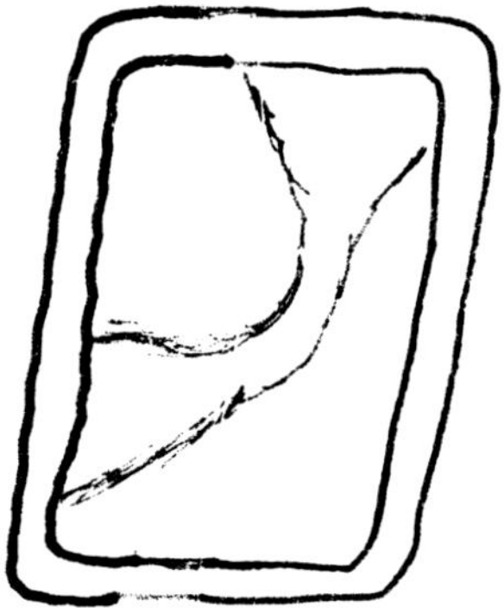

Mirror

Sloping Cave markings

The White Cove.

At the other end of the quarry is the White Cove. It was said to be of considerable size in 1888 and is again beginning to open up. It was filled in after a 'family of skeletons' was found here who had probably starved to death.

Entrance to the Sloping Cave 2000

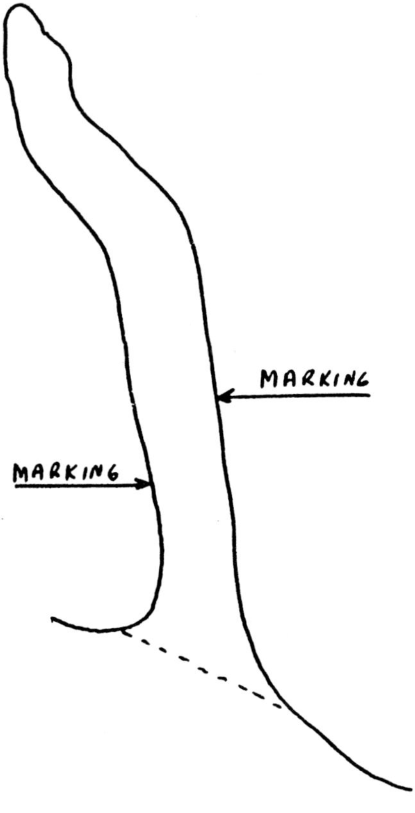

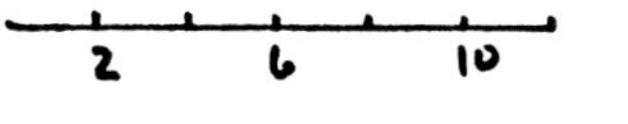

Plan of the Sloping Cave

Entrance to the Gasworks Cave

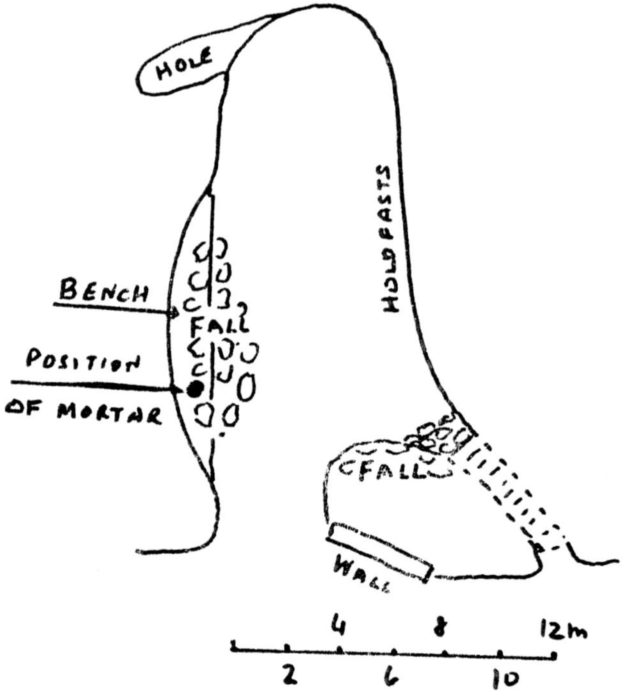

Gasworks Cave Plan

Gasworks Cave

Finally at the back of the remains of the Macduff Gasworks is the Gasworks Cave. Owing to coastal erosion access to this Cave is mainly at low tide.

The Cave is 20 metres in length, about 4 metres broad and over 3 metres in height. This cave was discovered in 1855 when workmen were building the Macduff Gasworks on the shore. The Cave was visited by Professor James Simpson in 1865 and 1866 and he described it thus:-

> There are no markings in this cave but there is a bench-like seam of rock as in Jonathan's Cave. At the end of the bench and next to the entrance is a mortar, globular in form in which traces of grain were found when discovered.
>
> The Cave is narrow and low-browed but dry. The floor has been paved with large boulders of lime-stone. Unfortunately they have all been tumbled about by people looking for treasure.

It is said that Professor Simpson took the corn that was in the mortar home and planted it in his garden near Edinburgh. It is interesting to note that after being in the Cave for untold generations, the corn grew. Although Professor Simpson described the Cave as dry, in recent years the Cave has become wet and a large fall of rock took place in 1959 covering the bench and mortar. There is a row of complete holdfasts on the east wall.

After the Gasworks had been demolished around 1970, the entrance of a small 'cave ' was found on the east side. It had been covered up at the gable-end of an outbuilding in the Gasworks. Inside the built up entrance was another wall and the Cave at the back of this was filled in. It is in the opinion of the author that this may have been another entrance to the Gasworks Cave.

Conclusion

At one time superstitious people believed that the 'Wemyss Caves contained supernatural beings in their darkest recesses' but now we know that they contain the finest records of Ancient Scotland.

The Society asks you to support them to 'Save the Wemyss Ancient Caves' in the Society's efforts. The Society will not be satisfied until the Wemyss Caves are protected and there is a safe access to them all.

The Society is working so that these Caves and their drawings will be there for future generations to come.

This is our Heritage......Help us to preserve it.

Blocked entrance to the Glass Cave 1996

References

Boucher, R. Jnr	The Kingdom of Fife	1899
Cunningham, A.S	Rambles Parishes Scoonie & Wemyss	1905
Deas, G.B	Kirkcaldy Burgh and Shyre.	1924
Geddie, J	Fringes of Fife	1865
Mackie andGlaister	Wemyss Caves. Fife	1981
Laing, T	Kindom of Fife	1951
Leighton, T	Fife Illustrated Volume 3	1840

Notes on:-

Royal Commission on Ancient & Historical Monuments of Scotland,

Inventory of Counties Fife, Kinross and Clackmannan 1933

Proceedings of Society Antiquities of Scotland Volume 11 1865

" "Sculptured Caves near Dysart" 1875

Old Maps

Coastal Erosion and the Big Hole 1996

Jonathan's Cave before the Grilles were inserted.

Ambry, Court Cave.
Used by the Covenanters during the open-air Conventicles in the 17th Century